BODY SYSTEMS

Eating and Digestion

Angela Royston

RIGBY
INTERACTIVE
LIBRARY

© 1997 Rigby Education
Published by Rigby Interactive Library,
an imprint of Rigby Education,
division of Reed Elsevier, Inc.
500 Coventry Lane
Crystal Lake, IL 60014

Interiors designed by Inklines and Small House Design
Illustrations by David Cook, except: Peter Stevenson, p. 17;
Peter Bull Art Studio, p. 11, p. 15 (left), p. 16, p. 21; John Bovosier, p. 12, p. 13.

Printed in the United Kingdom

00 99 98 97 96
10 9 8 7 6 5 4 3 2 1

Library of Congress Cataloging-in-Publication Data
Royston, Angela
    Digestion / Angela Royston.
      p.   cm. – (Body systems)
Includes bibliographical references and index.
Summary: Describes the various parts of the body and how they aid in digestion,
including the teeth and tongue, stomach, intestines, and kidneys.
      ISBN 1-57572-098-1 (library)
      1. Digestion – Juvenile literature [1. Digestive system. 2. Digestion.]
I. Title. II. Series: Body systems (Crystal Lake, Ill.
QP145.R69 1997
612.3 – dc20
                                                                    96-27554
                                                                       CIP
                                                                       AC

Acknowledgments
The publisher would like to thank the following for permission to reproduce photographs:
Colorific, p. 29; Oxford Scientific Films, p. 5; Science Photo Library, p. 9 (right), p. 18, p. 21, p.
22, p. 23, pp. 24–5, p. 25 (right), p. 27 (both); Telegraph Colour Library, pp. 8–9, pp. 28–9;
Tony Stone Images, p. 4, p. 7, p. 14. Commissioned photographs p. 6 and p. 13: Trevor Clifford.

Every effort has been made to contact copyright holders of any material reproduced in this book.
Any omissions will be rectified in subsequent printings if notice is given to the publisher.

Note to the Reader
Some words in this book are printed in **bold** type. This indicates that the word is listed in the
glossary on pages 30–31. This glossary gives a brief explanation of words that may be new to you.

Visit Rigby's Education Station® on the World Wide Web at http://www.rigby.com

Contents

Food, Your Body's Fuel

Your body is like a very complicated machine, and it needs fuel to keep it going. Cars burn gasoline to run their engines. Your fuel is food. It gives you energy to move around, grow, and stay healthy. Special parts of the body, which together make up the **digestive system**, turn the food you put in your mouth into the kind of fuel your body can use.

Digestive system

The process of **digestion** begins in your mouth. When you eat something, you first chew it with your teeth. Then you swallow it. The food is pushed down to your **stomach,** where it churns around for two or three hours. Then it passes into a long tube called the **intestines.**

There the food is gradually broken down into smaller pieces. The useful parts, which are called **nutrients,** are absorbed into your body. The rest winds its way along to the end of the tube and is finally forced out of your body when you defecate.

► *This athlete drinks water with glucose, a kind of sugar, to give him energy during a marathon run. He will certainly need plenty of energy to finish this 26-mile race!*

Delivering food to the cells

Nutrients pass into your blood, which takes them all around your body. Every part of your body, even your digestive system, is made up of tiny living **cells.** Most of these cells are too small to see without a microscope. Each kind of cell does a particular job in your body. Some form bones, some form skin, some form the heart, and so on. Each cell needs a supply of fuel, in the form of food, to stay alive and keep doing its special job.

Did you know?

We need to eat a huge amount of food to stay alive and healthy. You could easily eat 172 pounds of potatoes, 57 pounds of sugar, 500 apples, 150 loaves of bread, and more than 200 eggs each year, not to mention all the pizzas, chocolate, and other food you may eat. Most people in Europe, North America, and Australasia probably eat about 77,000 pounds of food during their lives — nearly 1,000 times the weight of your body.

◀ A drop of blood, magnified thousands of times to show the red blood cells. Blood is made of different kinds of cells. One of blood's many jobs is to take food to all the other living cells in the body.

You Are What You Eat

When you are hungry you may want to eat a huge pizza with lots of toppings. Your eyes see cheese, tomato, mushroom, and pepperoni, but did you ever realize that your body is really crying out for **carbohydrates**, **fats**, **proteins**, **vitamins,** and **minerals?** You need proteins to grow and replace old, worn-out cells, carbohydrates and fats to give you energy, and vitamins and minerals to keep your body working properly.

Energy-rich food

You use most of the food you eat for energy. Carbohydrates—bread, pasta, rice, and potatoes—are the best sources of energy. Sugar is a carbohydrate that gives energy quickly—but often too quickly. Fat provides the most energy of any food for its weight—but you can easily take in too much of it. The biggest sources of fat in food are meat, oil, milk, and milk products. Spreads such as mayonnaise are also mainly fat.

Body-building food

Meat, fish, eggs, cheese, and beans all contain lots of proteins. These complicated substances help you grow. As you grow taller, your **muscles, lungs, heart,** and so on have to grow bigger too, and protein helps you build these parts. Also, your body cells do not live as long as you do. Most live only a few weeks before they die, but the body uses proteins to make new cells to replace them.

▶ *Pizza looks and smells delicious. It also contains* nutrients *that give you energy, help you grow, and keep you healthy.*

Vitamins and minerals

Food contains small amounts of vitamins and mincrals. There are several kinds of vitamins, and most are known by letters of the alphabet. Carrots, fish, and corn, for example, contain vitamin A, which helps keep skin and eyes healthy. Eggs, whole grains, and meat contain various kinds of vitamin B, which help the body's cells. Milk and cheese contain the minerals calcium and phosphorus needed for healthy bones and teeth. Dark green vegetables provide the iron needed by the blood.

◄ *Fresh fruit and vegetables are rich in vitamin C. This vitamin helps your skin to keep healthy and is essential to prevent a disease called scurvy, which causes bleeding in the gums, skin, and joints.*

Did you know?

You use up energy even when you are asleep! Energy is measured in calories (cal) and you burn 55 cal every hour that you sleep. Sitting uses 75 cal/hr and walking 200 cal/hr. Climbing stairs burns 800 cal/hr, but could you do it for that long? To replace all that burned-up energy you could eat a plate of spaghetti (400 cal), a portion of baked beans (178 cal), two slices of bread (160 cal), and one or two oranges (40 cal).

Digesting Food

How does your body turn the food you eat into the nutrients it needs? It digests the food, or breaks it down into smaller and smaller pieces. The digestive organs are so thorough that they can reduce food to **molecules**, which dissolve in water and pass into the blood. Your body uses **digestive juices** and special proteins called **enzymes** to break down your food.

In the kitchen

Cooking makes food taste better and kills any germs in it. But it also helps the process of digestion by breaking down the cell walls a little so that the food is easier to chew. Food must be heated to a high temperature before cooking starts to break it down. The human body is able to digest, or break down, food at much lower temperatures.

In the body

Acids in your mouth and stomach mix with the food and help to break it down. Enzymes are the magic ingredients that allow your body to digest uncooked food. They allow the **chemical reactions** that break down the food to take place. Acids in the stomach also kill off **bacteria** and other germs. Later in the digestive process, however, the body actually relies on other bacteria to help break down undigested food.

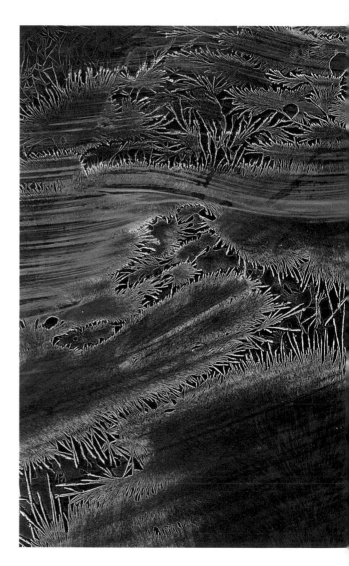

▲ *Acids are very powerful. This metal has been worn away and broken down by acid. In your stomach, acids work with enzymes to break down food.*

▲ This picture of an enzyme was drawn by a computer.

Did you know?

Our bodies are made of the same substances as our food, but the acids that help to break down food do not digest our own stomachs. This is because the stomach is protected by a thick coating of sticky mucus that shields it from the acidic digestive juices.

Your Digestive System

The digestive system is a production line for processing food. As food travels from the mouth to the **anus**, it is churned, squeezed, and squirted with various digestive juices. The main parts of the digestion machine are the mouth, the **esophagus**, the stomach, the small intestine, and the large intestine. The whole tube is called the **alimentary canal,** and it is about 33 feet long. Various **glands** keep it supplied with juices and enzymes.

Moving food along

The alimentary canal is made of muscle—not muscle like that in your arms and legs, but smooth muscle. Its main job is to push the food along in much the same way that you push toothpaste along by squeezing the tube. This squeezing action is called **peristalsis,** and the wave-like movements of the muscle keep the food moving. This means that you can swallow even while standing on your head!

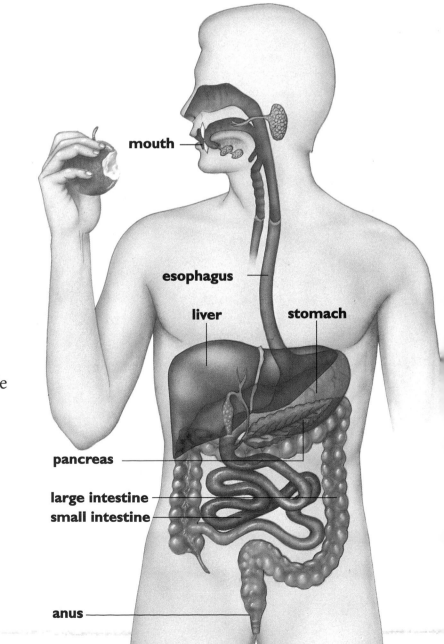

mouth

esophagus

liver

stomach

pancreas

large intestine

small intestine

anus

▶ *The main parts of the digestive system.*

One-way gates

Wherever one part of the digestive system connects to the next part, there is usually a kind of round **valve** called a **sphincter.** Valves are one-way gates. They make sure that food keeps going in the right direction. So, if you touch your toes, the food in your stomach will not come back up to your mouth. You can, of course, still be sick. The anus, at the end of the line, is also a sphincter. It controls when the waste from food leaves your body.

Glands

Glands all along the alimentary canal provide the different chemicals needed at each stage of digestion. The **liver** and the **pancreas** are two very large glands. The stomach also is lined with millions of tiny glands, which make acid and enzymes.

▼ *The muscles of the intestines contract (shorten) and relax to push the food along.*

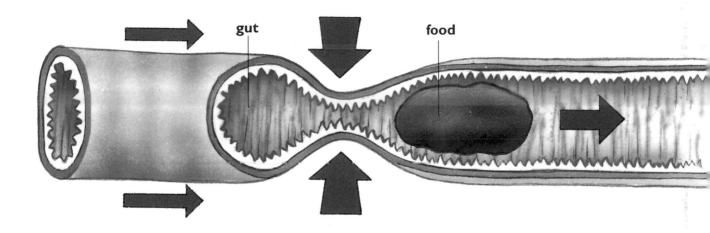

gut   food

Did you know?

It takes about a day for food to pass all the way through the alimentary canal. A few seconds after you swallow food, it lands in your stomach where it stays for about three hours (longer for a big meal). It takes another 20 hours or so to pass through the intestines. Some food is digested much faster than other kinds of food. Food that is very hard to digest, such as some nuts, may take two or three days to make the whole journey.

Your Teeth

The process of digestion begins in the mouth. Teeth break up the food and grind it into smaller pieces. Only the lower jaw can move, so the lower teeth work against the upper teeth to bite and chew. Teeth have to be hard and tough to do this job. They are covered with a layer of ename—the hardest substance in the body.

Mechanical breakers

Teeth are like precision tools. They are shaped to do different jobs. You use the incisors, the eight flat, sharp front teeth, to cut or slice food. The four long canines, fang-like teeth on each side of your incisors, are good for gripping and tearing.

Your eight premolars tear and grind the food. The twelve large flat molars at the back of your mouth grind the food down into small pieces. Adults have 32 teeth altogether, but the first set, the milk teeth, consist of only 20.

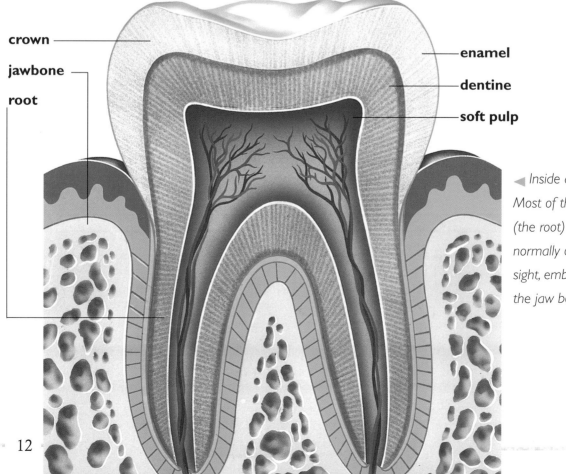

crown

jawbone

root

enamel

dentine

soft pulp

◄ *Inside a tooth. Most of the tooth (the root) is normally out of sight, embedded in the jaw bone.*

Tooth decay

Even after you have swallowed, tiny particles of food remain in your mouth. They cling to your teeth and gums and cause **decay.** Sugar does the most damage. Bacteria in the mouth change sugary food particles into acids that attack the teeth's enamel. First, small holes appear in the enamel, then larger ones in the **dentine** beneath. If the decay is allowed to reach the soft **pulp** in the center, it will cause agonizing toothache. The only way to prevent tooth decay is to brush your teeth at night and in the morning and always after eating sweet things.

incisor

canine

premolar

▲ A person has two sets of teeth. The first set begins to fall out at about the age of six. Bigger, permanent teeth (shown in blue) push through the gum to take their place.

◀ To avoid tooth decay, you have to brush your teeth soon after eating sweet things.

Did you know?

George Washington, the first president of the United States, probably did not clean his teeth properly. They were so rotten his dentist pulled them out and made him a false set carved from a hippopotamus tusk. Celluloid, the first plastic, invented in 1868, was soon used to make false teeth. Unfortunately, the teeth melted when their wearer drank hot liquid!

Your Mouth

The first thing you notice when you put something in your mouth is what it feels and tastes like. Rotten or poisonous food often tastes bad—a good warning not to eat it. Your tongue moves the food around your mouth, and the process of digestion begins. As well as being broken down into smaller pieces by chewing, food has to be mixed with saliva (spit) to make it soft and mushy enough to be swallowed.

Tongue

The tongue is a big muscle, which makes the mushy, chewed food into a ball ready for swallowing. The tongue is also mainly responsible for the sense of taste. The tip, edge and back are covered with about 3,000 taste buds, but there are just four different kinds of them. Every taste is a mixture of sweet, salty, sour and bitter. Each taste bud reacts to just one of the four basic tastes and your brain learns to recognize the mixture.

Pure chocolate is very bitter. It is mixed with sugar to make it more tasty. But if you lick chocolate with just the tip of your tongue, all you will taste is sweetness. You have to push the chocolate to the back of your tongue to get the full flavor.

▶ *Licking an ice cream quickly tells you how good it tastes.*

Saliva

Taste buds do not react to dry food. It has to be mixed with saliva first. There are three pairs of salivary glands that supply the mouth. One pair makes the sticky liquid that mixes with the chewed food and two pairs make an enzyme that starts the chemical process of digestion. It turns some starches into sugar. Saliva is also slightly **antiseptic;** that is, it attacks germs that enter your mouth.

▼ Taste-buds are concentrated around the edge and back of the tongue. Each part of the tongue responds to a different kind of taste.

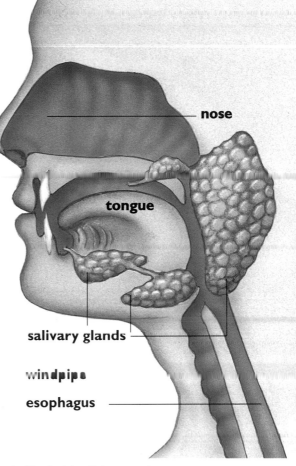

nose

tongue

salivary glands

windpipe

esophagus

▲ The inside of the mouth.

bitter

sour

sour

salt

salt

sweet

Did you know?

You make over a quart of spit every day and you swallow it all the time. See how long you can last without swallowing— or dribbling. It won't be more than a minute or two. You make more saliva at some times than at others. When you see food you really want to eat, your mouth begins to "water" with saliva, getting ready to eat. When your body needs more liquid, however, your mouth becomes dry and you feel thirsty.

Swallowing

When you chew a lump of food, you reduce it to a small packet of mush. Your tongue pushes this mush toward your throat, and you automatically swallow it. The mush slides into your throat and down your esophagus, helped along by peristalsis. The act of swallowing causes special flaps to close the passages into your nose and lungs, so the only way the food can go is down to your stomach.

Swallowing

The roof of the mouth is called the **palate**. It is hard in the main cavity of the mouth but becomes soft at the back. When chewed-up, mushy food touches the back of your throat, you swallow automatically.

The soft palate moves up and closes the air passage from the nose. At the same time, a flap called the **epiglottis** closes the windpipe to the lungs. You cannot breathe for one or two seconds while you swallow.

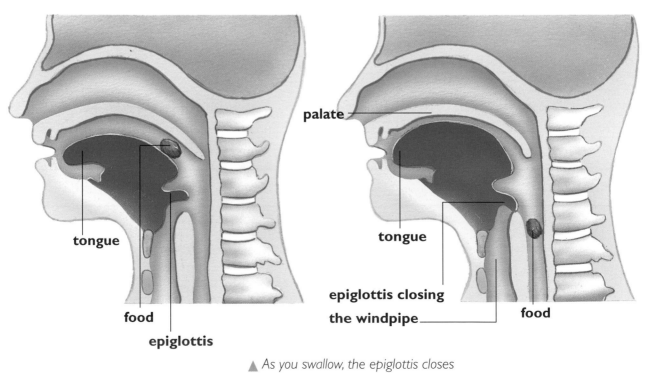

tongue

food

epiglottis

palate

tongue

epiglottis closing the windpipe

food

▲ *As you swallow, the epiglottis closes off the windpipe to prevent choking.*

Choking

There are two causes of choking. Sometimes you swallow a very large lump of food by mistake. Most such lumps make their way down the esophagus by themselves. You may even feel them doing so. What if something gets stuck in your throat? It will usually be dislodged when you cough. Sometimes food "goes down the wrong way." The epiglottis doesn't do its job and a crumb or two gets into the windpipe. Again, coughing helps to clear the windpipe.

▲ Sometimes, swallowing can be hard work!

Did you know?

When you swallow a bite of food, it enters your esophagus, a tube that runs from the back of your throat to your stomach. Muscles in the esophagus gradually push the bite of food down to your stomach in a wavelike action. It takes about 10 seconds for each wave to travel from the top of your esophagus to the bottom!

Your Stomach

The stomach is a stretchy, muscular bag which both stores food and helps to digest it. It acts a bit like a big electric blender, churning the food around and turning it into a liquid, called chyme. The valve at the lower end of the stomach empties the chyme, bit by bit, into the small intestine. It takes about three hours for an ordinary meal to pass through the stomach. A very large meal can take up to six hours.

Food mixers

The stomach wall has three layers. Beneath the outer coat is a layer of muscle that contracts every few seconds to move the food around.

The innermost layer, the stomach lining, is covered with tiny glands. Some secrete mucus, and others secrete **hydrochloric acid** and as soon as food reaches the stomach these **gastric juices** pour over it. Hydrochloric acid kills germs and mixes with the food. Enzymes begin to digest protein. Some sugar is absorbed into the blood, but the main process of digestion takes place in the small intestine.

◄ The lining of the stomach is covered with mucus to protect it from the acid it produces. In this magnified photo most of the slime has been removed so that you can see the folded wall of the stomach below.

Vomiting

Many things can make you sick to your stomach, such as illness, bad smells, and food that is too rich or sugary. Normally, the valve between the esophagus and the stomach lets food go into the stomach but prevents it from going back up again.

When you are sick, however, the muscles in your belly and **diaphragm** squeeze your stomach and the valve to the small intestine closes so that the contents of the stomach are forced up the esophagus and into your mouth.

► *The stomach is shaped roughly like a boxing glove. Bands of muscle squeeze it in different directions, churning up the food inside it. The inner lining is ridged and pitted.*

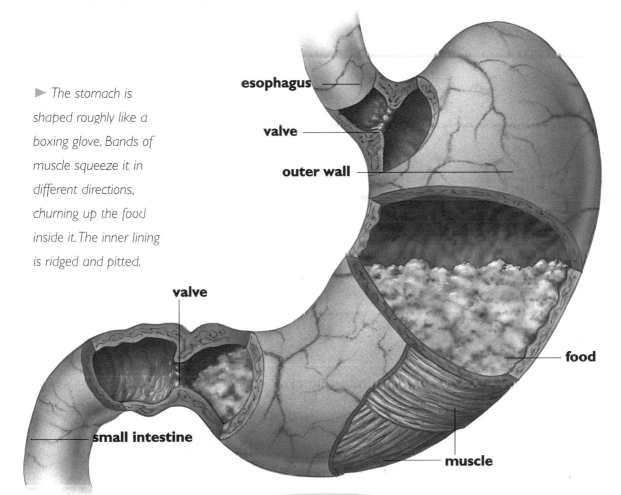

esophagus

valve

outer wall

valve

small intestine

food

muscle

Did you know?

Do you sometimes have a hollow feeling in your stomach when you are hungry? Your stomach is small when it is empty. As you eat, it stretches, perhaps to two or three times the volume, depending on how much you eat. Then you feel full. The human stomach can hold up to three pints — much less than some animals. A cow's stomach can hold up to 47 gallons!

Your Small Intestine

The small intestine is not actually small—it is from 13 to 17 feet long and more than an inch wide. It has three parts. In the first part, called the **duodenum, alkaline** digestive juices break down the chyme into smaller molecules and neutralize any acids. The breaking down continues in the middle part, the **jejunum.** By the time the molecules reach the third part, the **ileum,** they have become small enough to move through the thin walls into the blood.

Sprayed with juices

The duodenum is about 10 inches long. Its juices neutralize acids in the liquid that arrives from the stomach. About halfway along the duodenum, a tube from the **gall bladder** and one from the pancreas come together and join the duodenum. Enzymes and digestive juices from the pancreas continue the process started in the stomach of breaking down proteins. They also attack the carbohydrates. **Bile** from the gall bladder breaks down fats in much the same way that dish soap does.

▶ The long tube of the small intestine is coiled into the space between the ribs and the pelvis. Small quantities of chyme pass into the small intestine through a valve at the end of the stomach.

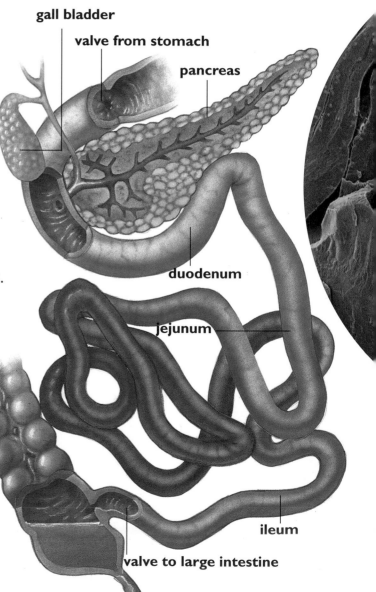

gall bladder

valve from stomach

pancreas

duodenum

jejunum

ileum

valve to large intestine

Absorbed into the blood

Food gets absorbed into the bloodstream mainly in the ileum. By the time the food gets there, proteins have been reduced to **amino acids,** carbohydrates to simple sugars, and fats into tiny fatty molecules.

They are now small enough to pass between the cells of the **villi** and through the walls of the tiny blood vessels into the blood itself. But before your body cells can use these nutrients, they go to the liver for processing.

▼ The walls of the villi in the ileum are so thin that food molecules can pass through them into the bloodstream.

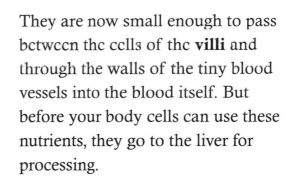

blood vessels

▲ The lining of the ileum is folded into tiny ridges covered with millions of tiny finger like parts called villi.

Did you know?
The small intestine provides an enormous surface through which food molecules can be absorbed. If you unravelled the entire tube, flattened out all the villi, and straightened out all the ridges, you would get a sheet of lining large enough to cover a ping-pong table, an area five times as large as that of the skin on your body.

Your Liver and Pancreas

The liver is the largest **organ** in your body. Together with a smaller organ, the pancreas, it helps your body to absorb food into the bloodstream. The liver weighs about 3.3 pounds and carries out more than 500 different jobs.

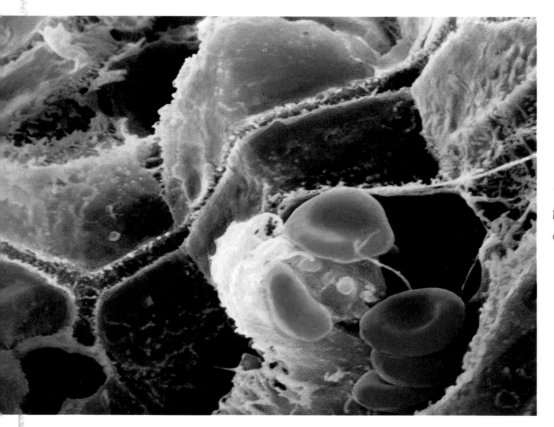

◀ This magnified photo shows the cells in the liver.

Processing food and waste

Blood rich with nutrients goes from the small intestine straight to the liver. If there is more digested food in the blood than the body needs, the liver changes the extra into glycogen, a kind of sugar, and stores it. It also stores some vitamins and destroys some poisons. It releases the right amount of nutrients into the blood.

The blood then travels on to the heart and lungs and, well stocked with food and oxygen, the blood is pumped to all the body's cells. The liver also cleans the blood. It removes dead red blood cells and waste products which have been produced by the cells. Some of the waste is made into bile and stored in the gall bladder.

lobes

stomach

◄ The liver has two large
round projections or lobes.
The tiny blood vessels from
the small intestine join up
to form a single vein.

vein from
intestines

artery from heart

gall bladder

The pancreas

The pancreas has two jobs. Every day it
makes about a quart of the digestive
juices that break down carbohydrates,
proteins, and fats in the small intestine.
It also produces two **hormones**—
insulin and glucagon. These control
the amount of sugar in the blood.
Insulin is produced when there is
too much sugar in the blood, and
glucagon when there is too little. A
diabetic person is one whose pancreas
does not make enough insulin.

▲ Diabetics inject
themselves regularly with
the insulin that their bodies
need but cannot produce.

Did you know?

**You could live without most of your stomach
but you could not survive without your liver. If only
part of the liver is removed, however, you will be all
right. Even if only a quarter remains, the liver can still
function and new cells grow so quickly that within
six to eight weeks the whole organ will be
as big as before.**

Your Large Intestine

The large intestine is about 6 feet long and makes a big loop around the small intestine. Indigestible parts of food, water, and minerals from the small intestine pass slowly through it. The mineral salts and much of the water are absorbed into the body and the remaining waste becomes a soft solid called **feces.** Feces are stored in the **rectum** until they are expelled from the body through the anus.

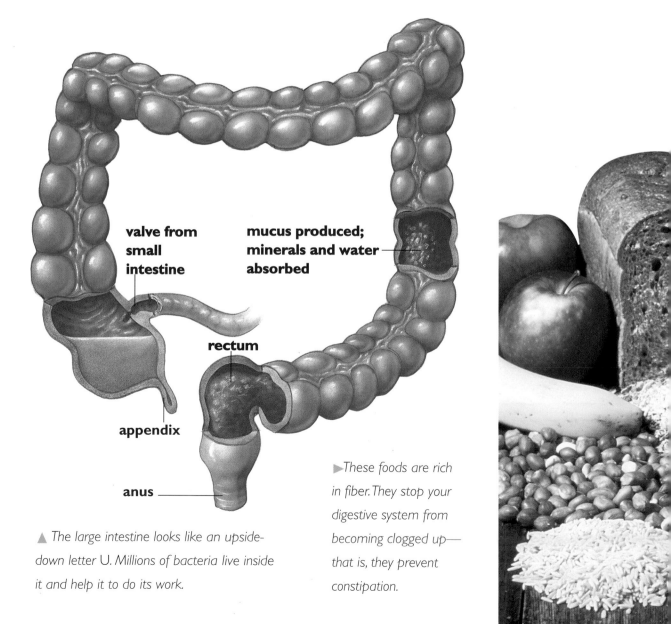

valve from small intestine

mucus produced; minerals and water absorbed

rectum

appendix

anus

▲ The large intestine looks like an upside-down letter U. Millions of bacteria live inside it and help it to do its work.

►These foods are rich in fiber. They stop your digestive system from becoming clogged up— that is, they prevent constipation.

Water

The fact that water is reabsorbed into the body saves you from having to drink so much. Not all the water is absorbed, however. About three-fifths of feces is water. Drinking plenty of liquid helps to prevent **constipation**, when the feces have become too dry and hard and are therefore difficult to expel. **Diarrhea** occurs when waste passes through the large intestine so quickly, there is not enough time for the water to be absorbed. If this happens, it is essential to drink extra liquid to replace the water that is lost.

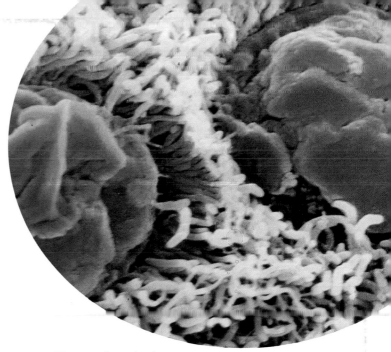

▲ These cells in the large intestine absorb water and make mucus.

Fiber and bacteria

Undigested food in feces consists of plant parts called fiber or roughage. It might seem surprising, but the more fiber you eat, the better your digestive system works. Fiber helps prevent constipation and many diseases. Feces also contain mucus, dead cells from the stomach lining, and millions of bacteria, most of which are also dead.

Did you know?

The appendix *is a dead-end organ in the digestive system. It appears to have no use at all, but human beings are not the only ones who have it. Monkeys, apes, and rodents have it, too. Although the appendix is useless, it can be dangerous. If it becomes inflamed, it causes terrible pain and must be removed.*

Your Kidneys and Bladder

You have two **kidneys,** one on each side of the body, just below the ribs. They do two main jobs. They filter the blood to remove a poisonous waste called **urea**, and they remove extra water from the blood. The urea and water form **urine** that drains into the **bladder.** It is stored in this stretchy, muscular bag until you get rid of it when you urinate.

Millions of filters

As the body's cells burn up food and energy, they produce waste (like a car's exhaust). The waste from carbohydrates and fats turns into water and carbon dioxide, which is breathed out through the lungs. The waste from protein, however, is turned into urea by the liver. It is carried in the blood to the kidneys.

Inside each kidney there are millions of tiny, twisting tubes and capillaries (very fine blood vessels). The blood passes through this network, where it is filtered. The purified blood is reabsorbed into the body. The urea and any unwanted water are left behind and trickle down into the bladder.

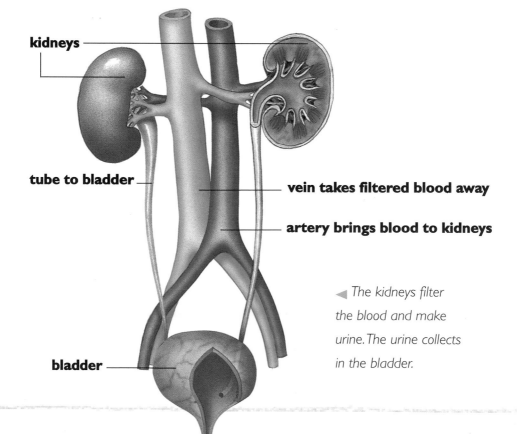

kidneys

tube to bladder

vein takes filtered blood away

artery brings blood to kidneys

bladder

◄ *The kidneys filter the blood and make urine. The urine collects in the bladder.*

Water control

The kidneys control how much water is lost in urine. They make sure the body retains just the right amount. The kidneys make about 2 quarts of urine a day. The more you drink, the more you urinate. But if you sweat a lot, you urinate less because you have lost some of the extra water through your skin. A valve, or sphincter, at the bottom of the bladder keeps the urine from escaping, but when the bladder is full, your brain realizes that you need to empty it. You can then decide when to relax the valve and release the urine.

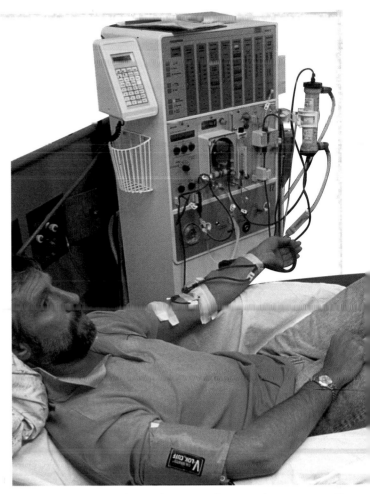

▲ Some people's kidneys do not work properly. Every few days they can hook up to this huge machine, which filters their blood.

Did you know?
Most of your body—about seven-tenths of your weight—is water. Four-fifths of the blood is water, and three-quarters of muscle is water. Your bones are one-quarter water. No wonder water is so important to the body! Most of your food—nine-tenths of all fruits and vegetables—is water, too.

◄ This magnified photograph shows the inside of a kidney.

27

Healthful Eating

Food can be unhealthful in two quite different ways. If it contains germs and the germs get into your stomach, you can become ill. Contaminated food can give you stomach pains, diarrhea, or a more serious illness. Your diet is the kind of food you usually eat. If your diet is poor, your body will not work as well as it should. This can lead to various diseases over the years.

Food and hygiene

Food should be kept clean and stored properly. Even food kept in the fridge should usually be eaten within a few days. Any food may contain germs, but cooking it properly kills most of them. The stomach juices usually kill the rest, provided there are not too many. It is also important to wash your hands before you eat.

A balanced diet

If you eat a variety of foods that provide all the nutrients you need in the right amounts, you are eating a balanced diet. By contrast, if you eat a lot of fatty, salty food, such as french fries and hot dogs, and not much fruit or fresh vegetables, you may well have health problems later in life. In adults, fat globules, called cholesterol, can gather in the arteries. This can cause **heart attacks** and other illnesses.

Food and energy

If you eat more fat than you need, the body stores it under your skin. Everyone needs some fat to stay warm, but too much weight puts an extra strain on the heart. It can be dangerous to be too thin, however. The body needs a good supply of food to give you the energy to enjoy yourself and to learn at school. The energy value of food is measured in calories. The actual number of calories you need each day varies according to your age, height, and sex, and how much exercise you are getting.

◄ It is important to wash your hands after going to the bathroom and before eating. Germs on your hands can easily get onto your food and make you ill.

▲ This man is jogging to help avoid becoming overweight. The best way for overweight people to lose weight is to eat fewer calories and to exercise more.

Did you know?

The heaviest person ever recorded weighed over 800 pounds when he died in 1983. He was Jon Minnoch who lived in Washington State. He weighed nearly five times the average weight of 167 pounds for men his age. Some wrestlers weigh over 485 pounds, three times as much as most other men.

Glossary

Acid Sour-tasting substance that can burn skin and wear down metals. The mouth and stomach produce acidic juices to help digest food.

Alimentary canal Long tube that joins the mouth to the anus. It consists of the esophagus, the stomach, and the small and large intestines. It allows food to pass slowly through the body while the nutrients are digested. Only the waste reaches the anus.

Alkali Substance that neutralizes an acid. The first part of the small intestine, the duodenum, is supplied with **alkaline** digestive juices.

Amino acids Basic building blocks that make up proteins.

Anus Valve or sphincter muscle at the end of the alimentary canal that controls the release of feces from the rectum.

Appendix Small, dead-end branch at the start of the large intestine.

Bacteria Single, living cells that function independently. They are so small that we can see them only through a microscope. There are millions of bacteria in the mouth and other parts of the body. Most are harmless, but some can cause disease.

Bile Juice made in the liver and stored in the gall bladder. It is released into the duodenum to break down fats into tiny droplets.

Bladder Stretchy, muscular sac that stores urine before the urine is expelled from the body.

Carbohydrates Substances found in food such as bread, rice, pasta, potatoes, and sugar. Carbohydrates provide the body with energy and are of two main types: sugar and starch. During digestion, starches are broken down into simple sugars.

Cell Smallest living unit. Each part of the body is built up of a different kind of cell.

Chemical reaction Process of change in which the molecules of two or more substances combine to form new substances.

Constipation Condition of having dry, hard feces that are difficult to expel.

Decay To rot.

Dentin Hard, yellow tissue that surrounds the **pulp, or innermost layer,** of a tooth.

Diaphragm Sheet of muscles below the lungs which contracts and relaxes to make you breathe air in and out.

Diarrhea Condition of having extremely liquid feces.

Digest Break up food into smaller molecules that can be absorbed into the blood and used by the body. The process of digesting food is called **digestion.**

Digestive juices Liquids made by glands that help break down food. Digestive juices contain enzymes and may be acidic, alkaline, or neutral.

Digestive system All the parts of the body that are used to digest food.

Duodenum First part of the small intestine. Juices from the liver and pancreas break down food that has passed into the duodenum from the stomach.

Enzymes Proteins made by the body that trigger chemical reactions, such as the breaking down of food, without themselves being changed.

Epiglottis Flap in the back of the throat that closes off the windpipe to the lungs.

Esophagus Tube that links the mouth with the stomach.

Fats Substances found in some foods, which the body uses as a source of energy. For example, foods such as eggs, milk, cheese, meat, and vegetable oils contain fats that provide a concentrated source of energy.

Feces Soft solid waste expelled from the body through the anus.

Gall bladder Small bag in which bile is stored before being released into the duodenum.

Gastric juices Juices produced by the lining of the stomach. They include enzymes and hydrochloric acid which break down food.

Gland An organ of the body that makes special substances such as hormones or digestive juices.

Heart Organ within the chest that pumps blood through the blood vessels to all the body's living cells.

Hormones Chemicals produced by glands and carried around in the blood to help control many of the body's processes. Insulin, for example, is a hormone that controls the amount of sugar in the blood.

Hydrochloric acid Strong acid normally present in dilute form in the stomach's gastric juices.

Ileum Third and last part of the small intestine.

Intestines The long tube that connects the stomach to the anus. It consists of two parts — the small intestine and the large intestine.

Jejunum Middle part of the small intestine.

Kidneys Pair of organs that filter blood to remove poisonous waste and produce urine.

Liver Organ of the body that processes digested food molecules and other chemicals in the blood. It is the largest organ in the body.

Lungs Two organs within the chest cavity that are used in breathing. When air is breathed into the lungs, the blood there absorbs oxygen from the air and releases carbon dioxide to be breathed out.

Minerals Chemicals, such as calcium and phosphorus, which the body needs to stay healthy.

Molecule Smallest part of a substance that can exist by itself and keep the properties of the substance. If a complex molecule is broken down it becomes two or more simpler substances.

Mucus Slimy liquid produced by particular parts of the body.

Muscle Bundle of fibers that shorten and get thicker to produce movement.

Nutrients Parts of food that the body needs for energy or to build new cells.

Organ Part of the body, such as the heart, which does a particular job. The stomach, intestines, pancreas and liver are the main digestive organs.

Palate Roof of the mouth. It is hard at the front and soft at the back.

Pancreas Large gland that produces digestive juices and enzymes to help digest fats. Juices from the pancreas are released into the duodenum. The pancreas also makes insulin, which controls the amount of sugar in the blood.

Peristalsis Contractions of the muscles of the esophagus and intestines which move food through the digestive system. The contractions pass like a wave along the tubes.

Protein Substance found in some foods that our bodies need to grow new cells and replace old ones. Proteins consist of carbon, hydrogen, oxygen, and nitrogen. Parts of the body, such as muscles, are made of protein.

Rectum Final part of the large intestine, before the anus.

Sphincter See **Valve.**

Stomach Muscular sac below the chest in which swallowed food is stored for a few hours while it is churned around and mixed with acidic digestive juices.

Urea Substance which when mixed with water in the kidneys forms urine. Waste protein from the cells is made into urea in the liver and carried in the blood to the kidneys.

Urine Liquid formed by the kidneys from urea and surplus water, stored in the bladder, and expelled during urination.

Valve Device that allows movement in one direction only. There is a round valve, called a sphincter, where one part of the alimentary canal to joins the next part.

Villi Tiny, finger-like projections about 0.3 inches long in the ileum lining. Villi absorb nutrients into the blood.

Vitamins Chemicals that the body needs in very small quantities to stay healthy.

Index

Further Reading

Parker, Steve. *Eating a Meal: How You Eat, Drink, and Digest.* Danbury, CT.: Franklin Watts, 1991.

Patent, Dorothy. *Nutrition: What's in the Food We Eat.* New York: Holiday House, 1992.

Reef, Catherine. *Eat the Right Stuff.* New York: Twenty-First Century Books, 1993.